Changing materials

A brief history

TODAY... New chemicals are being invented at the rate of 400,000 a year. Already, nearly 20 million substances are known... 1911 William Burton shows how to use heat to turn petroleum into new materials... 1909 Leo Baekeland, in America, develops the first widely used plastic. It is called bakelite... 1908 German chemist Fritz Haber discovers how to make fertilizer from nitrogen in the air. Charles Cross, in England, invents cellophane, a transparent plastic... 1891 Edward Acheson, in America, discovers how to make the new material called carborundum... 1886 Alfred Nobel, Swedish chemist, discovers how to make a smokeless explosive... 1877 English inventor Joseph Swan patents the process of making rayon from plants. It is the first plastic ever made... 1856 Henry Bessemer, a British engineer, finds a new way to make steel cheaply... 1844 German chemist Otto Wallach finds out how to remove natural oils from plants. This allows the creation of the perfume industry... 1807 Sir Humphrey Davy, an English chemist, separates the pure metals sodium and potassium from rock by using electricity... 1774 French chemist Antoine Lavoisier proves that burning needs only a part of the air, which he calls oxygen... 1772 Wilhelm Scheele, a Swedish chemist and pharmacist, isolates oxygen and calls it fire air... 1660 Irish chemist Robert Boyle discovers that air is important in burning and that small animals cannot live without air...

Dr. Brian Knapp

Word list

These are some science words that you should look out for as you go through the book. They are shown using CAPITAL letters.

ACID
A liquid with a sour taste that combines with many other substances.

BOILING POINT
The temperature at which a liquid bubbles and turns into a gas.

BRITTLE
A substance that cracks when struck sharply.

BURN
To give off heat through a flame.

CARBON
A black substance found in all living or once-living things.

CHEMICAL
A pure substance, often a liquid, that combines with other substances.

CONDENSE
To change from a gas to a liquid.

CRYSTAL
A solid with a regular shape.

DILUTE
To add water to a liquid.

DISSOLVE
To break up into small particles that seem to disappear into a liquid.

DYE
A substance that stains materials with a color.

EARTHENWARE
Pottery that has been heated to over 800°C to make it hard.

ELECTROPLATING
Using electricity to put a thin metal coating on a material.

FUEL
A substance that gives out considerable amounts of heat as it burns.

GAS
A form of a substance in which the particles are free to move around.

IRON
A metal that rusts in damp air.

LIQUID
A form of a substance in which particles can slide past one another.

MAN-MADE FIBER
A threadlike material made from chemicals.

MATERIAL
A useful substance.

MELT
To change from a solid to a liquid.

METAL
A substance that has a shiny surface and that conducts electricity.

OPAQUE
A substance that will not let light pass through it.

ORE
A rock containing a lot of metal.

PLASTIC
A range of materials made from the substances in oil, gas, wood, or coal.

POWDER
A ground-up form of a solid.

REACT, REACTION
The combining of two chemicals to create new substances.

RUST
The reddish surface coating that develops on iron and steel in damp air.

SOLID
A form of a substance in which all of the particles are locked tightly together.

STEEL
A mixture of iron and carbon.

SULFUR
A yellow substance often found near volcanoes.

TARNISH
A surface coating that develops on some metals when they are exposed to the air.

TRANSPARENT
An object that is see-through.

WATER VAPOR
Water in the form of a gas.

Contents

How do substances change?

Substances can be changed in many ways. Some changes can be reversed, while others cannot.

We are always changing the **MATERIALS** around us. For example, every time we eat some food, switch on a light, or go on a bus, materials are being changed.

If you look around the room you are sitting in, you will see many more examples of change. The chairs may be covered in **MAN-MADE FIBERS**; the computer could have a **PLASTIC** case; the desk lamp may have a **METAL** base. None of these things occurs naturally—all have to be made by changing or combining different materials.

Iron filings

Sulfur powder

▲▶ (Picture 1) Reversible change. If you mix iron filings with powdered sulfur, you get a yellow mixture containing dark-gray iron specks. If you push a magnet into the mixture, you can remove all of the iron. Mixing sulfur and iron is a reversible change.

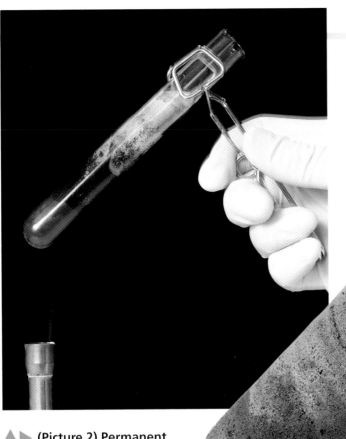

(Picture 2) Permanent change. If you mix iron filings with powdered sulfur and then heat them with a very high heat, the sulfur and iron combine. A new substance has been made. You cannot separate the iron and sulfur in this new substance. This is an example of an irreversible change.

Similarly, when you mix some solids together, for example, powdered **SULFUR** and **IRON**, you can separate them again by using a magnet (Picture 1).

Permanent, irreversible changes

Many changes cannot be reversed. If you heat the mixture of sulfur and iron, for example, a new material will be formed. A magnet could not separate iron from sulfur in this new material (Picture 2).

The importance of change

Here are some of the common ways of changing substances permanently:

▶ They can be heated.
▶ They can have electricity passed through them.
▶ They can be added to a liquid or to other substances.

Using methods like these, iron is removed from rock, gas is separated from oil, colored **DYES** are made from coal, and grapes are turned into wine. The possibilities for making new substances are endless and are part of the excitement of science.

There are two very different ways we change materials. One is reversible, and the other is permanent, or irreversible.

Reversible changes

In the case of reversible changes the material is not permanently altered.

For example, when you boil water, you make **WATER VAPOR**. But when you cool the vapor down again, the **LIQUID** water reappears. So although you have changed the water from liquid to **GAS**, it is still water.

Summary

• Some changes to materials can be reversed.
• Often, when materials are combined, a new material is produced.
• Many of our most useful materials are made by permanently changing other substances.

Heating

When a substance is heated, irreversible changes often occur.

When a **SOLID** is heated, it may **MELT** and become a liquid. That is what happens to wax, for example. It is a reversible change. But many substances change before they get hot enough to melt. These are irreversible changes.

Firing clay

Since ancient times people have known that clay changes when it is heated. Some of the earliest things made were pottery, formed by shaping clay while it was wet (Picture 1), then heating it in an oven.

If clay is dried in the air, it will become hard (Picture 2). But this is not an irreversible change; if you wet dry clay, the clay will become soft again. However, if the clay is heated in a very hot oven, called a kiln, at temperatures of over 800°C, then changes will take place that make the clay hard and **BRITTLE**.

(Picture 2) Allowing the clay to dry out in the sun will make the clay hard. Adding water, however, will make it soft again. This is a reversible change.

(Picture 1) Moist clay is easy to form into a shape. At this stage it is very soft and is quite unsuitable for use as a container or an ornament.

(Picture 3) Heating the clay in a special oven to over 800°C makes the clay hard. It is now pottery. Adding water will not soften it. This is an irreversible change.

Adding water will not soften this clay. The heat has caused the clay to change irreversibly into a new material with new properties (Picture 3). This kind of pottery is called **EARTHENWARE**. Higher temperatures make stoneware and porcelain.

Cooking food

Every substance is affected by heat at a unique temperature. Most foods will change when they are heated to the **BOILING POINT** of water (100°C). That is why boiling is an important form of cooking.

Some foods that contain flour will also cook at this temperature (to make steamed puddings, for example), but other foods containing flour will not cook properly until they are heated to a higher temperature.

Bread and cakes need to be cooked at temperatures of about 180°C to 200°C.

The changes that take place when heating foods are far more complicated than those in clay. You can easily see some of the changes that occur when an egg is boiled (Picture 4).

The egg contains both white (which, uncooked, is almost colorless) and yolk (which is yellow). As the egg is heated, the yolk changes from a liquid to a solid. The white changes even more dramatically, from a liquid to a solid and also from **TRANSPARENT** to **OPAQUE**. None of these changes can be reversed.

(Picture 4) A boiled egg and a loaf of bread are common examples of irreversible changes made by heating.

Summary

- When substances are heated, changes often occur well below the temperatures at which the substances melt.
- Every substance changes at a unique temperature.
- Heating can cause substances to change from liquids to solids or to become harder.

Burning

When something burns, gases, and sometimes ash or soot, are produced.

When something **BURNS**, it breaks down into new substances that cannot be brought together later to remake the original substance again. Here are some examples of burning.

When a candle flame burns, most of the wax turns into a vapor and disappears (Picture 1).

When a match burns through the wood of the matchstick, it leaves only a thin, burned stump behind, and all that remains of a coal or wood fire is a small pile of ashes.

Burning produces gases

Where have the wax, coal, and wood gone? Nearly all of it has been turned into a gas, and it has literally disappeared into the air. When something burns, it gets very hot and combines with the oxygen in the air to make new gases. One of these gases is called carbon dioxide.

◀ (Picture 1) As a candle burns, the wax turns partly to vapor and also burns. The gas carries tiny particles of soot up with it. The soot glows almost white hot, and that is what actually gives off the light we see. To prove there is soot, just place a plate a few centimeters above the flame. After a few seconds the soot will be left on it.

Burning releases heat

Anything we burn for heat is called a **FUEL**. Fuels include wax, wood, coal, and oil.

A fuel gives out heat when it changes into a gas, and the gas combines with the oxygen of the air.

Burning leaves ash or soot

Because burning changes a solid fuel into a gas, the amount of solid becomes smaller (Picture 2). That is why the amount of material left when burning is finished is much smaller than the amount of fuel at the start of burning. The material that remains is mostly made of **CARBON**. It may be made of tiny particles that are carried up into the air with the flame. We call these tiny particles of carbon soot. That is what happens when a candle burns.

If material remains behind after burning is complete, we call it ash. It is what you get from a bonfire or a coal fire.

▲ (Picture 2) As a fire burns, it sends up gases into the air. When it has gone out, the fire leaves behind a gray ash and pieces of partly burned wood.

Summary

- When a fuel burns, it changes mainly into a gas.
- During burning tiny particles of carbon may be carried up as soot.
- Any carbon that remains after burning is called ash.

Changes with water

Some substances change permanently when they are mixed with water.

Some substances combine with water to form new, hard materials called **CRYSTALS**. Crystals form in the following way: A fine **POWDER** of the substance is mixed with water. The water and the powder combine and form a new material, which sets into long, thin, needlelike crystals. These crystals are too small to see without a very powerful microscope. But as the crystals grow and interweave, they make a strong, hard substance. Once the crystals have grown, the water cannot be removed from them.

The two most common materials of this kind are called plaster of Paris and cement.

Plaster of Paris

Plaster of Paris is a fine, white powder. It is made from crushing and then heating a rock called gypsum. It is used to make molds and plaster wallboards in houses or to fill cracks in walls. It is also used to make plaster casts (Picture 1). The material used to encase a broken arm or leg is plaster of Paris.

(Picture 1) Plaster of Paris used to make a mold of family feet.

(Picture 2) What happens in a concrete mix.

1

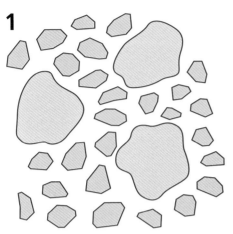

Sand and gravel are mixed together.

2

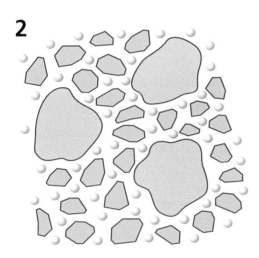

Cement and water are mixed in.

3

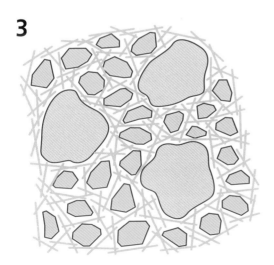

The substances in the cement combine with the water to form needle-shaped crystals that set hard and lock the sand and gravel in place.

(Picture 3) A bridge being made of concrete.

Cement

Cement is a much harder material than plaster of Paris. It is made by first grinding up limestone and clay. These materials are heated in a furnace, then ground once more. This is cement. When water is added, the cement and water combine to make interlocking crystals.

Cement is usually used to bind some other materials together. That is how it is used in concrete (Pictures 2 and 3). Concrete is made from sand, cement, and small stones called gravel. These ingredients are all thoroughly mixed together, and water is added.

Because the cement has been mixed in with the sand and gravel, when the cement crystals grow, they surround these materials, locking them into place.

Summary

- Some substances combine with water to make new hard materials.
- When plaster of Paris or cement mix with water, they form interlocking crystals that are hard to break.

Rusting and tarnishing

Rust is a change that affects ordinary iron and steel in water or damp air.

Being exposed to the air is a dangerous thing for many common metals. That is because many metals combine with the oxygen and other gases in the air to create a new material.

Rusting

Iron or **STEEL** is especially liable to combine with oxygen. When this happens, the surface of the metal changes from shiny gray to dark-brown. The surface develops pits and bumps, and flakes of **BRITTLE** material form (Picture 1). It is called **RUST**. It is an irreversible change.

▼ **(Picture 1)** Anything made of ordinary steel will rust when placed in a damp environment. This old horseshoe is completely covered in rust. When looked at closely, rust is seen to be made of sheets of flaking material.

▲ **(Picture 2)** If a steel nail is half-covered in water, the part of the nail in the water quickly becomes rusty. The water naturally contains oxygen, so the combination of water and oxygen attacks the nail. The yellow material at the bottom of the glass jar is rust that has already fallen from the nail.

Iron or steel will not combine with oxygen if the air is dry, however. That is why nails stay bright and shiny indoors. But as soon as water is present and the air gets damp, both metals rust quickly (Picture 2).

When iron combines with oxygen gas in the air, the material produced is made of both iron and oxygen, so it takes up more space. The more the iron or steel rusts, the thicker the coat becomes, until it finally breaks away as a flake of rust.

Tarnishing

Many metals do not combine with oxygen as dramatically as iron and steel. Instead, they develop a thin, dull coating that actually seals the metal and protects it from further attack. This coating is called **TARNISH**. The green color that develops on the surface of copper (Picture 3) and the brown and black stains on silver (Picture 4) are good examples of tarnishing.

Unlike rusting, which continues until all the iron is used up, tarnishing does not harm the metal underneath.

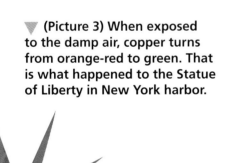

▼ (Picture 3) When exposed to the damp air, copper turns from orange-red to green. That is what happened to the Statue of Liberty in New York harbor.

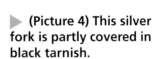

▶ (Picture 4) This silver fork is partly covered in black tarnish.

Summary

- Many metals combine with oxygen and other gases in the air.
- When iron and steel combine with oxygen and water, it causes rusting.
- Most metals combine with oxygen to form a thin, colored, dull coating called tarnish.

Electroplating

Electricity can break materials apart and release pure metals.

Most materials are made of two or more substances that are locked together with chemical "glues." A rock, for example, is made of many substances locked together. But if you can find the right method, it is possible to "unglue" the substances and release them. One method is to pass an electric current through the material. That is how some metals are removed from rocks.

Using electricity, it is also possible to get metals to form a thin, even coating over other materials. That is called ELECTROPLATING.

Many things are electroplated with shiny metals: from the silver on cutlery to the chrome on taps or the gold on brooches (Picture 1).

How electroplating works

It is quite easy to electroplate the surface of a metal object with copper using a chemical called copper sulfate or even common salt (a teaspoonful in a glass of water), a copper wire, and a bicycle battery.

In Picture 2 a key is being electroplated with copper. The key forms part of an electric circuit. A wire is connected from the key to the negative side of the battery. A copper wire is connected to the positive side of the battery. The other end of

(Picture 1) Plating is a common way of getting a smooth, even finish. The tap (left) has been plated with a very shiny metal called chromium; Above, a real orchid flower has been plated with gold and made into a brooch.

this wire is stripped. It will be the source of copper for electroplating. Alternatively, a small strip of copper can be used (Picture 3). Once the circuit is connected, the key, metal strip, or any other metal object you choose starts to become plated with copper.

How electroplating works: As electricity flows from the battery and through the liquid, copper moves through the liquid. It plates the object connected to the negative side of the battery.

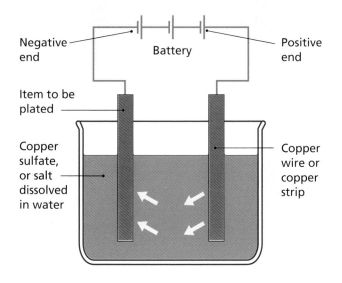

Negative end

Battery

Positive end

Item to be plated

Copper sulfate, or salt dissolved in water

Copper wire or copper strip

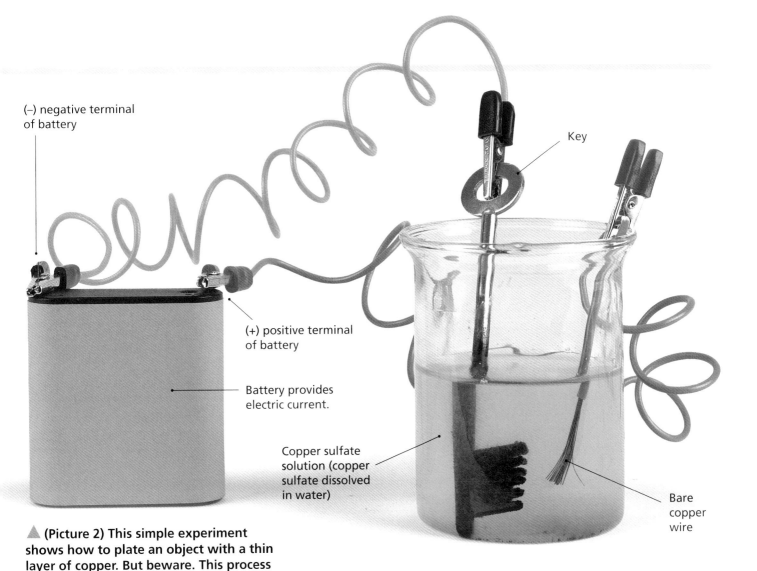

(–) negative terminal of battery

Key

(+) positive terminal of battery

Battery provides electric current.

Copper sulfate solution (copper sulfate dissolved in water)

Bare copper wire

▲ **(Picture 2) This simple experiment shows how to plate an object with a thin layer of copper. But beware. This process is not reversible, so once the copper has plated the object, you will not be able to rub it off; so don't use anything valuable.**

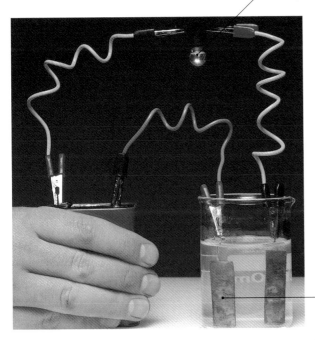

Flashlight bulb

The strip collects copper on its surface and becomes bright orange.

Summary

- **Electricity can be used to change substances.**
- **Electroplating transfers a metal from one object to another.**
- **A special liquid is needed for electroplating.**

◀ **(Picture 3) This is the same experiment, but salt dissolved in water is used instead of copper sulfate. A bulb has also been connected into the wiring to show that electricity is flowing. Notice that the liquid bubbles as the plating takes place. A key can be used instead of a metal strip.**

Using acids

Some common liquids have special properties. These liquids are called acids, and they always cause irreversible change.

What do lemon juice and vinegar have in common? If you taste them, they are both sharp and sour. The sourness is because they contain special substances called **ACIDS**. Acids are liquids that readily combine with many other substances and change them.

There are many natural acids. All of the citrus fruits contain acid, for example. It is called citric acid. Vinegar, which is usually made from apples, grapes, or malted barley, contains acetic acid. These natural acids are all weak acids and do no harm to people.

Scientists can also make very strong acids, however, and they can be harmful. Car batteries, for example, contain a powerful acid called sulfuric acid.

Acids that fizz

Acids can combine, or **REACT**, with other substances to release a gas. If vinegar is poured onto a piece of chalk, for example, it will fizz dramatically as a gas is released (Picture 1).

If you add a seltzer tablet (the sort sold by druggists as fizzy antacid tablets) to water, gas bubbles are produced. You can see the gas bubbles fizzing in the water, and you can hear them breaking the surface. The gas is a new

▲ (Picture 1) When vinegar is added to a piece of chalk, fizzing occurs. The gas is carbon dioxide.

substance, and it escapes to the air, so an irreversible change has taken place.

To see how much gas is produced, put two seltzer tablets into a bottle with about half a cup of water in it, and quickly put a balloon over the top. As the gas is produced, the balloon will inflate (Picture 2).

The seltzer tablet contains two substances, both in solid form. One is baking powder, and the other is a solid form of citric acid. (Both substances are harmless, which is why you can drink the fizzy liquid as a cure for indigestion.) When they are in solid form, they will not combine. When the tablet goes into the water, the baking soda and the acid dissolve and then combine to produce

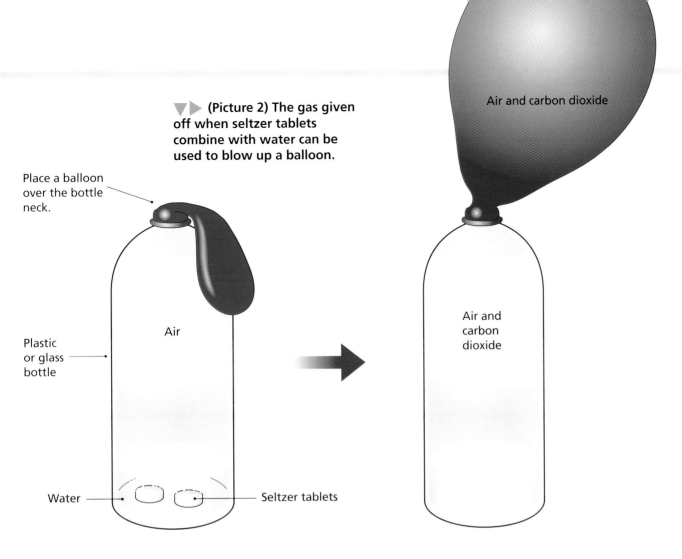

(Picture 2) The gas given off when seltzer tablets combine with water can be used to blow up a balloon.

Air and carbon dioxide

Place a balloon over the bottle neck.

Plastic or glass bottle

Air

Water

Seltzer tablets

Air and carbon dioxide

carbon dioxide gas, which expands into the air and blows up the balloon.

If you ask an adult to put a seltzer tablet and a small amount of water into a plastic 35mm film canister, you can see an even more dramatic demonstration of the power of this chemical reaction (Picture 3). Ask them to partly fill the canister with water, and quickly put on the snap-top lid. Then shake, stand well back, and wait for the pressure of the gas to blow the lid off the canister!

Summary
- **Acids combine with many other substances.**
- **Strong acids can be dangerous to handle.**
- **Some reactions give off gases.**

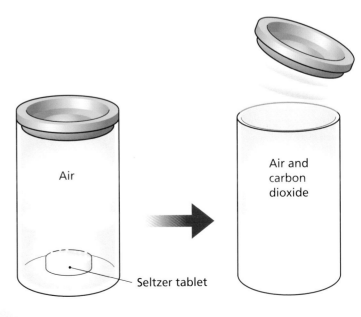

(Picture 3) If you ask an adult to place a seltzer tablet and water in a film canister, the top will blow off like a cannon.

Air

Air and carbon dioxide

Seltzer tablet

Changes that bring danger

Some changes are dramatic. You should always read the label on chemicals to prevent accidents.

We use **CHEMICALS** around the home every day. To do their job properly, some chemicals have to work very hard and are very strong. Here are just two examples of chemicals that can cause unexpected and dangerous results if used improperly.

DANGER Caustic soda "eats" (dissolves) grease, which means it could also dissolve your skin. That is why the bottle says that users should wear gloves. It also gives off dangerous fumes. So the bottle tells you not to breathe the fumes. And it dissolves aluminum, which is why the bottle warns you not to put it near things made of aluminum.

▶ ▼ (Picture 1) Caustic soda crystals (right) for use in drains; caustic soda used on oven cleaning pads (below). Notice that gloves are being used to protect the skin.

Caustic soda

Caustic soda is a chemical sold for cleaning ovens and drains by dissolving grease (Picture 1). It is an irreversible change. Caustic soda is far too powerful to use ordinarily inside the home. Here we show you just why you must treat this chemical with respect.

Caustic soda and water

To begin any reaction, caustic soda must be added to water. When the crystals are added to water, they **DISSOLVE** and give out enormous amounts of heat and an unpleasant gas. The hot liquid then dissolves the grease. After a while the dissolved material can be washed away.

Caustic soda and aluminum

Aluminum is a metal that is used to make, among other things, drink cans, cooking pans, and pie plates. In normal use no changes take place when aluminum is used to hold liquids.

However, this is what happens when caustic soda is poured into an aluminum pie plate (Picture 2). First the liquid begins to fizz (Picture 3). As you have seen before, fizzing means that two substances are combining and giving off a gas.

◀ (Picture 2) An aluminum pie plate before caustic soda is poured into it.

NOTE The demonstration shown was done by a chemistry teacher using safety gloves and eye protection in the safety of a laboratory in a secondary school. It is here to show the dangers of misusing chemicals. This demonstration must never be done at home.

▼ (Picture 3) The fizzing that occurs when caustic soda is poured into the pie plate.

The fizzing is so violent that it hides what is happening. But when the fizzing stops, it is clear that the caustic soda has eaten its way right through the aluminum pie plate (Picture 4). The whole bottom has gone.

▼ (Picture 4) Within a few seconds the bottom of the pie plate has been eaten away.

Bleach

We use bleach to clean our toilets and get rid of germs. Bleach is quite safe if used properly. But bleach combines with any kind of tissue, which is why it is always best to use bleach with household gloves—so there is no risk of spilling it onto the skin. And make sure it doesn't drip onto the carpet and other fabrics.

Slowing reactions with water

If a dangerous chemical does spill onto your skin, remember that chemicals are less active when they are **DILUTED**. That is why accidental spills should be diluted with lots of water.

Summary

- Some substances combine in a dangerous way. That is why it is vital to read the label before using any chemical.
- Some reactions give off poisonous fumes.

Making plastics

Plastics usually start off as brown crude oil. To get plastics from oil, the oil has to be split apart.

Ever wondered what goes on among all of the pipes and towers of an oil refinery? The answer is that most of the towers are designed to separate the parts of the oil by boiling it to make new materials (Picture 1).

Oil is a mixture

When oil comes out of the ground, it is a brown liquid. It is not just one substance, but a mixture of many substances. To get the substances to separate, they need to be heated.

When you heat a mixture, it boils, and the substances turn into gases. Each substance has its own **BOILING POINT**, so all you have to do

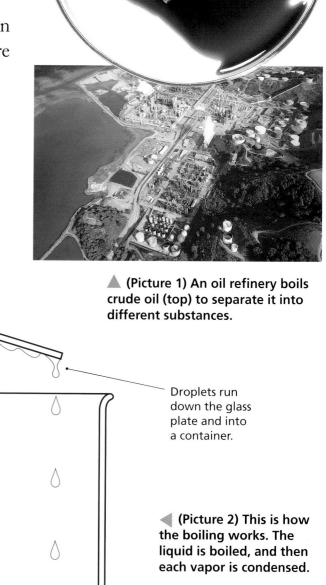

▲ (Picture 1) An oil refinery boils crude oil (top) to separate it into different substances.

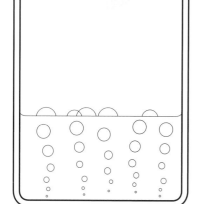

Heating a liquid mixture causes the liquid to begin to boil and give off vapors. The mixture of vapors then rises.

Other vapors rise.

One part of the vapor condenses on the plate, and droplets of liquid form.

Droplets run down the glass plate and into a container.

◀ (Picture 2) This is how the boiling works. The liquid is boiled, and then each vapor is condensed.

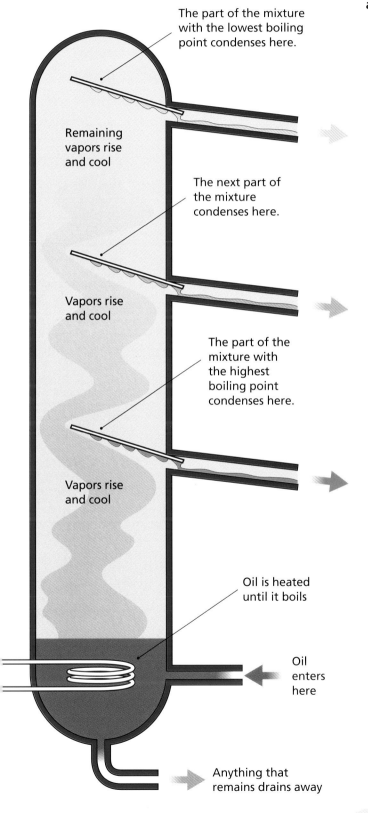

The part of the mixture with the lowest boiling point condenses here.

Remaining vapors rise and cool

The next part of the mixture condenses here.

Vapors rise and cool

The part of the mixture with the highest boiling point condenses here.

Vapors rise and cool

Oil is heated until it boils

Oil enters here

Anything that remains drains away

(Picture 4) Common plastics polythene (above) and polystyrene (right).

is to let the gases cool (Picture 2), and they will **CONDENSE** into liquids again. If you do this in a tall tower (Picture 3), then the temperature will be highest at the bottom and lowest at the top. So the substance that boils at the lowest temperature will condense at the top of the tower, while the liquid that boils at the highest temperature will condense near the bottom of the tower. Then it is simply a matter of collecting the liquids as they condense. Many of these liquids can be used to make plastics.

Making plastics

Plastics are made by making millions of particles join into long chains. This is an irreversible change.

A huge number of plastics can be made by arranging for the particles to join in different ways. What happens depends on which material is used as a supply of particles. Common plastics include polyethylene, vinyl (PVC), and polystyrene (Picture 4).

Summary
- Plastics are made from crude oil.
- Plastics are made by getting materials in the oil to recombine into long chains.

Making iron

Iron is one of the most useful materials, but it starts out inside rock. Releasing it requires heat and chemical reactions.

How do people get gray iron metal out of hard brown rock? The answer is to cause the rock to change.

The first people to discover how to do this began the period called the Iron Age. They were probably using some iron-rich lumps of rock as the stones to contain their fire. As the fire burned, the stones must have got hotter and hotter until the rock started to soften, and the iron flowed out. As the iron solidified, they found that pounding on it with another stone would change its shape.

In this way they discovered that the secret of getting iron from rock is to heat it. You can't do this with most iron-bearing rocks, only with those that have exceptionally large amounts of iron in them. Such rocks are called ORES. And even with ores, you can't get a very pure form of iron.

That explains why you don't see people getting iron from hearths today. Instead, they use giant towers called blast furnaces.

The blast furnace

A blast furnace (Picture 1) is a chemical factory designed to let pure iron flow out of rock. This is an irreversible change.

To do this, two things are needed: The rock must be hot enough for the iron to melt, and unwanted substances must be separated from the iron.

Millions of tons of iron are produced each year, so the amount of ingredients going into the furnace is huge. They are all tipped in at the top: iron ore (which is iron combined with oxygen), coke (a smokeless form of coal made mostly of carbon), and limestone. The coke is then set alight, and air is pumped in at the bottom to stoke the fire.

Inside the furnace all kinds of chemical reactions take place. The coke and the iron ore become white hot. The carbon from the coke combines with the oxygen from the iron ore, leaving the iron behind as pure metal. The limestone combines with other, unwanted substances and, being less dense than iron, floats on the melted iron. Finally, the pure iron is allowed to flow from the bottom of the furnace (Picture 2).

Summary

- Iron is found naturally combined in rocks.
- Heating iron ore with coke and limestone releases the iron.

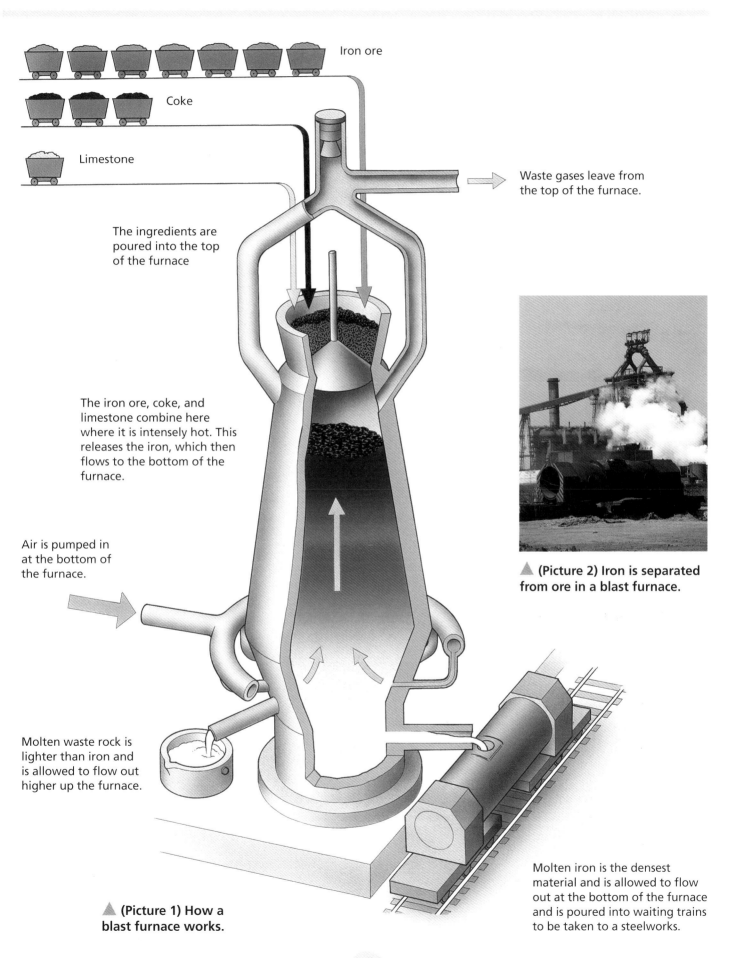

Iron ore

Coke

Limestone

Waste gases leave from the top of the furnace.

The ingredients are poured into the top of the furnace

The iron ore, coke, and limestone combine here where it is intensely hot. This releases the iron, which then flows to the bottom of the furnace.

▲ (Picture 2) Iron is separated from ore in a blast furnace.

Air is pumped in at the bottom of the furnace.

Molten waste rock is lighter than iron and is allowed to flow out higher up the furnace.

▲ (Picture 1) How a blast furnace works.

Molten iron is the densest material and is allowed to flow out at the bottom of the furnace and is poured into waiting trains to be taken to a steelworks.

Index

Science Matters!

Grolier Educational

First published in the United States in 2003 by Grolier Educational, Sherman Turnpike, Danbury, CT 06816

Copyright © 2003
Atlantic Europe Publishing Company Ltd.

All rights reserved. No part of this publication may be reproduced, stored in a retrieval system, or transmitted in any form or by any means—electronic, mechanical, photocopying, recording, or otherwise—without prior permission of the publisher.

This product is manufactured from sustainable managed forests. For every tree cut down at least one more is planted.

Author
Brian Knapp, BSc, PhD

Educational Consultant
Peter Riley, BSc, C Biol, MI Biol, PGCE

Art Director
Duncan McCrae, BSc

Senior Designer
Adele Humphries, BA, PGCE

Editor
Lisa Magloff, BA

Illustrations
David Woodroffe

Designed and produced by
Earthscape Editions

Reproduced in Malaysia by
Global Color

Printed in Hong Kong by
Wing King Tong Company Ltd

Picture credits
All photographs are from the Earthscape Editions photolibrary.

Library of Congress Cataloging-in-Publication Data
Knapp, Dr. Brian J.
    Science Matters! / [Dr. Brian J. Knapp].
        p. cm.
    Includes index.
    Summary: Presents information on a wide variety of topics in basic biology, chemistry, and physics.
    Contents: v. 1. Food, teeth, and eating—v. 2. Helping plants grow well—v. 3. Properties of materials—v. 4. Rocks and soils—v. 5. Springs and magnets—v. 6. Light and shadows—v. 7. Moving and growing—v. 8. Habitats—v. 9. Keeping warm and cool—v. 10. Solids and liquids—v. 11. Friction—v. 12. Simple electricity—v. 13. Keeping healthy—v. 14. Life cycles—v. 15. Gases around us—v. 16. Changing from solids to liquids to gases—v. 17. Earth and beyond—v. 18. Changing sounds—v. 19. Adapting and surviving—v. 20. Microbes—v. 21. Dissolving—v. 22. Changing materials—v. 23. Forces in action—v. 24. How we see things—v. 25. Changing circuits.
    ISBN 0-7172-5834-3 (set)—ISBN 0-7172-5835-1 (v. 1)—ISBN 0-7172-5836-X (v. 2)—ISBN 0-7172-5837-8 (v. 3)—ISBN 0-7172-5838-6 (v. 4)—ISBN 0-7172-5839-4 (v. 5)—ISBN 0-7172-5840-8 (v. 6)—ISBN 0-7172-5841-6 (v. 7)—ISBN 0-7172-5842-4 (v. 8)—ISBN 0-7172-5843-2 (v. 9)—ISBN 0-7172-5844-0 (v. 10)—ISBN 0-7172-5845-9 (v. 11)—ISBN 0-7172-5846-7 (v. 12)—ISBN 0-7172-5847-5 (v. 13)—ISBN 0-7172-5848-3 (v. 14)—ISBN 0-7172-5849-1 (v. 15)—ISBN 0-7172-5850-5 (v. 16)—ISBN 0-7172-5851-3 (v. 17)—ISBN 0-7172-5852-1 (v. 18)—ISBN 0-7172-5853-X (v. 19)—ISBN 0-7172-5854-8 (v. 20)—ISBN 0-7172-5855-6 (v. 21)—ISBN 0-7172-5856-4 (v. 22)—ISBN 0-7172-5857-2 (v. 23)—ISBN 0-7172-5858-0 (v. 24)—ISBN 0-7172-5859-9 (v. 25)
    1. Science—Juvenile literature. [1. Science.] I. Title.

Q163.K48 2002
500—dc21
                                                        2002017302